What is Cold Capping?

A GIRL'S GUIDE TO SAVING YOUR HAIR AND SURVIVING AGGRESSIVE CHEMOTHERAPY

Cold Capping 101: What every Girl should know: Who is trying to save their HAIR. While maintaining their Quality of LIFE during Aggressive Chemotherapy...The Secrets they aren't telling you.

Author: Sherri Paden
Illustrator: Sherri Paden
2/20/2020

Cold Capping 101: A Girl's Guide to Saving Your Hair and Surviving Aggressive Chemotherapy

Dedication Page...

This book is dedicated to my mom, Mrs. Denise Michelle Paden. Thank you for teaching me so much and loving me unconditionally. I Love You Dearly.

Also, to my son, Victor Alan Richeson, Jr...I am so very Proud of you each and every day. I am so Proud of the responsible young man that you have become, at the young age of 30. I love you with all of my heart...Love Forever, and Always, Mom...

Forward: This book will only work for patients who have

NOT already had chemo treatment therapy...This cold

capping guide will NOT work if you have already

started your chemotherapy but will still help with

avoiding Chemo Brain during the duration of your cancer

treatments.

My intent is to sell this book in order to get Grants to

Help women Get their own Cold Caps...I found 1 Grant

out there but that is not enough. I am writing this book

to help women and to Change the Mind Set of Cancer

Patients...This model has worked in London England for

over 2 Decades...That is 20 Years Ladies...Why are we so reluctant to try this, and so behind the times?

Introduction:

Hello there, my name is Sherri Paden and I decided that I would write a book when I was asked repeatedly why I was not losing my hair while was on Chemo. Another reason that I decided to write this book is because I discovered that I found a remedy to NO scalp HAIR LOSS DURING CHEMOTHERAPY...I have Cracked the Science on this cold capping thing...This was a clinical trial...that I have conducted on myself from conducting Extensive Research, Getting Family Financial

Support, and Online Support from Breast Cancer Patients. In addition to that...Trial and Error from 9 Months to a year (3 Self Trials Total).

A Little About Me:

I am a 1st Grade Teacher of 26 Years and I teach at an Elementary School at Prince George's County Public School, in Hyattsville Maryland. I am also a Native Washingtonian, which means that I was born and raised in our Nation's Capital, of Washington D.C.

My Diagnosis:

I was diagnosed with triple negative, invasive, carcinoma, breast cancer, and started my research on Cold Capping in July, of 2019. It is now, February of 2019. So now I am writing this book for all of the ladies who have in-boxed me about not wanting to feel vain about keeping your hair during this process…Don't' feel guilty about this because:

This hair process is about: The Quality of Life Ladies, and that is ALL about YOU!!!!

Your mind set and quality of life are also very important while going through this process. You have to make sure that you stay and remain positive throughout this entire process. I decided to write this book because I would hear lots of patients/ladies saying "I don't like the way that I look, or I don't look in mirrors anymore". Well ladies...YOU, are the ones who have inspired me to write this book as well. These steps worked for me and I am no scientist, but I do have a Degree in one of the Sciences, and I do know how to conduct a 3 Trial Scientific Experiment on MYSELF...

Back to my diagnosis, I caught it early, I guess. When it was removed (the tumor) it was 2.2cm... from being 2.5 cm that was noted and recorded in my previous Lab Work.

Women and their Quality of Life:

I felt that the quality of life that I wanted to have was important to me and I did not want to look different or lose my hair. It's not that important to everyone and each and every one of us has our own Cancer Patient Story to tell. Mine just happens to be on saving your hair, eyebrows and eyelashes. Your facial hair, and Cold Capping.

In writing this book... I Obviously have NO CHEMO BRAIN...I'm writing a freaking book!!! Go figure. Yeah, GOOGLE that ONE – (Chemo Brain) Because, I am still afraid to Google, "What is Chemo Brain?"

Book Dedication: I am dedicating this book to the Love of my Life (Rick) who shall remain somewhat Anonymous (Due to his Profession) for literally saving me emotionally, financially and Physically during my Very Long Days of Extensive Treatments...Some of my treatment days were 5 to 8 hours. Due to Long

Cold Capping Sessions of Pre and Post Cooling before and after

each treatment at the Hospital. It is like a (5-hour day) work

shift.

Also, thank you to my wonderful son, Victor Richeson Jr., and

his beautiful new wife Dominique Richeson. And All of the

wonderful 1st Graders, their parents and the Staff at Woodridge

E.S. in Maryland. I also want to thank my son's father Victor

Richeson Sr., and Joan and Andrew Richeson my ex-in – laws

who have always shown me LOVE and Support throughout my

life... Yes, Ex's can get along!!!!

I also want to dedicate this book to my 1st Grade Students of SY

2019-2020, for accepting me, when I missed a lot of days and for always staying so sweet, and thoughtful whenever I came back to school. The students knew, that I was taking, a kind of medicine, that would make me sick, so I had to stay home some days. I needed their help, in the classroom at times...and that's how I got a little help from my 1st Grade students on some days that I was really weak.

This book is also dedicated to My Dad, Mr. Teddy Paden, my stepmom Francis Black, my 4 Brothers Cimerron Trent Paden, Terron Paden, Nicholas Paden, and my deceased Brother Arron (may GOD rest his soul). My brother Arron Paden passed away in a car accident while going back to the Air Force. We love, and miss you, brother. Also, to my Uncle Sonny Marcus and Aunt Olivia in Philadelphia. And last, but not least...to my good

Children's Literature Author/friend Gwendolyn Evans- Orange.

Who would always tell me, how smart I was, and that I should

write a book. Well here I am, and now I have a topic that I am

passionate about, and that topic is Cold Capping. I hope that

you enjoy it and learn a lot from reading my book.

Sincerely,
Sherri M. Paden

TABLE OF CONTENTS:

CHAPTER 1
WHAT IS COLD CAPPING?

Medical Cold Caps are Cold caps that are offered in the Hospital. Some Cold Caps have been approved here in the USA and they do work if done correctly. This process is very expensive and costs $2,200.00. They ask for $700.00 up front and then $900.00 as a final payment for 8 treatments. If you don't want to go that route, then you will need to research where to find DRY ICE in the area that you live in. The Cold Cap machines at the Hospital, works as follows; 30 min. precooling, 1 ½ hours while getting infusion, and then 1-hour ½ Post Cooling is done at the hospital.

To do List:

*Research Cold Caps, they are offered at Some Hospitals.

*Plan 3 months ahead. It's hard, I know. Chemo has to start immediately according to the Doctor's...I will Explain...

*Purchase 5 to 6 Gel Caps on Online $60.00 each- They sellout often and quick. Contact me for brand names if needed.

*Always follow your doctor's advice, but also be an advocate for yourself as well. Listen to your BODY!!!!

Cold Capping Your Eyelashes and Eyebrows

What is cold capping and how do you do it? Cold Capping is the process of freezing your hair follicles so that the chemo does not get a chance to reach the brain. You can cold cap to -32', do not go below this temperature...Dry Ice will give you this -32' result. When you come home to cold cap...the temperature can be taken down a notch just to cool your head down...Even positive numbers are ok for capping at home...10 degrees or −10 it's all okay. Cold capping the face is also very important as well. On chemo day, your body will be hot like fire so cool it down by cooling your head.

You can do this at home, by putting the cold caps

in the Freezer, but be sure to set it on the highest

temperature the day before Chemo treatment...

This will ensure that your caps will be frozen for the

following day. Then turn down the freezer's temperature

on day 3, when you no longer need to have a cold cap

after treatments. I will clear up all misconceptions about cold

capping in Chapter 5 and a step-by-step guide on what to do

treatment days.

Picture Gallery:

Remember to...Eat Healthy foods that you can stomach.

Small front part and hair is always flat on hot days....

Started Chemotherapy Treatment - December of 2019.

No hair loss...Post 2nd Treatment AC Adriamycin (Red Devil)

Infusion.

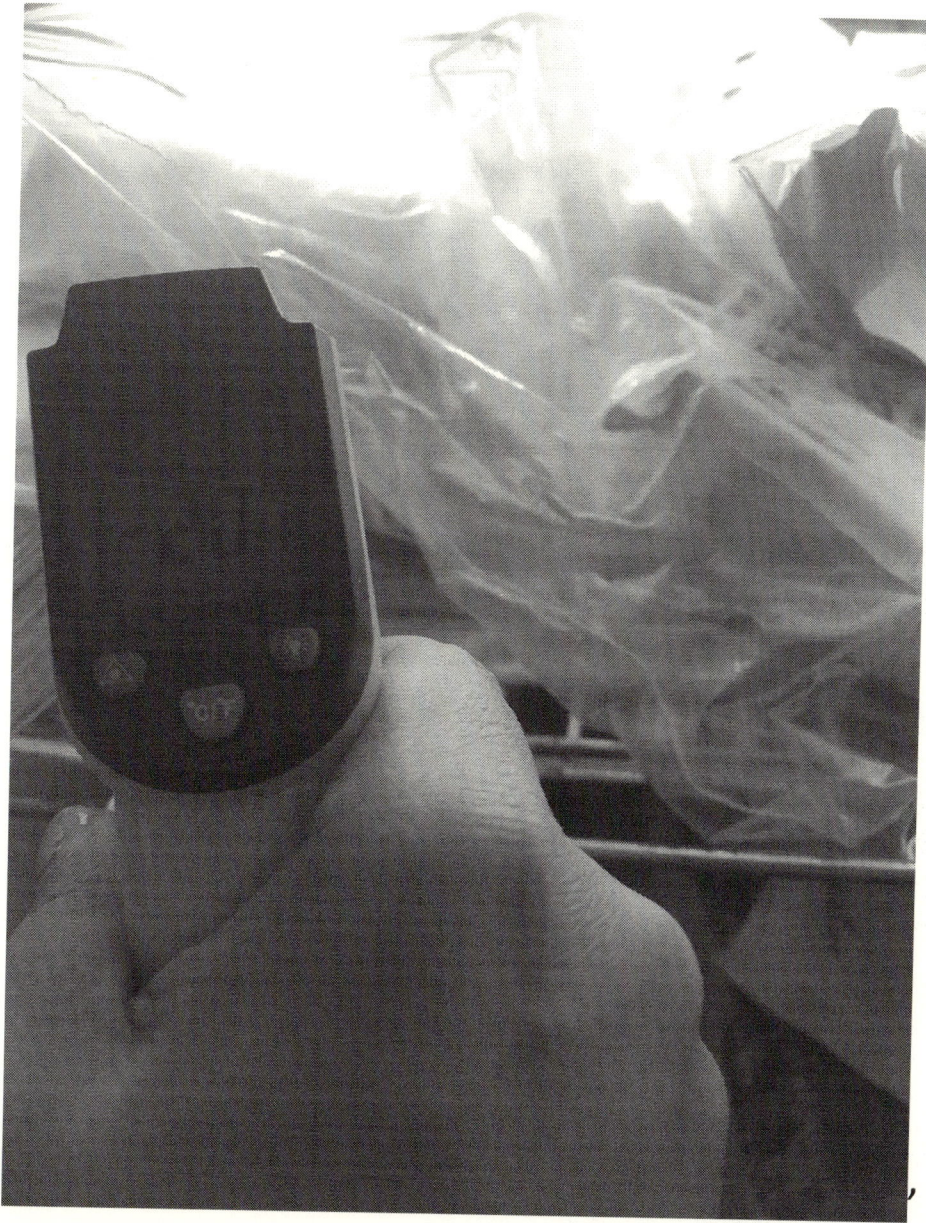

Dry Ice in the freezer kept on the highest setting on Capping days...

Me Capping Post infusions /Day 2 Capping Post infusion.

Daily vitamins take 2 a day of the Pure Graviola.

Take 1 per day of the Bamboo Extract and the Horsetail Hair
Vitamins.

Oh, great my hair is still here.

Important: Soft Toothbrush and Toothpaste with baking soda. Also, get your teeth cleaned before your first infusion treatment.

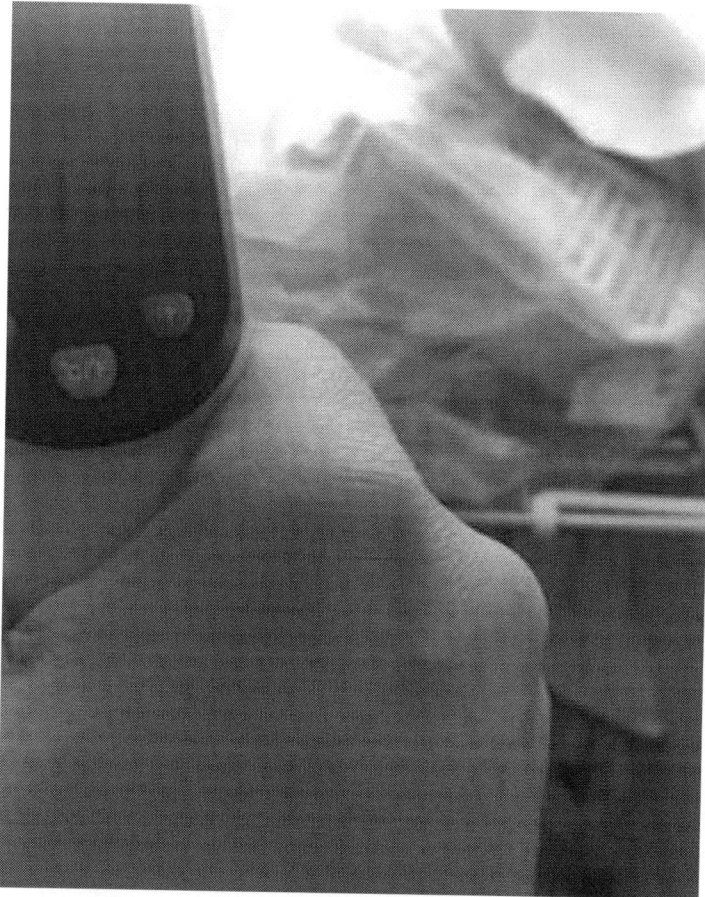

Laser temperature gauge.

AC Adriamycin (Red Devil) Chemo

Post 2nd Chemo Treatment AC infusion.

Still no hair loss.

AC Adriamycin (Red Devil) Chemo

Put a %100 silk scarf under cap at home.

So that there is minimal contact with your scalp.

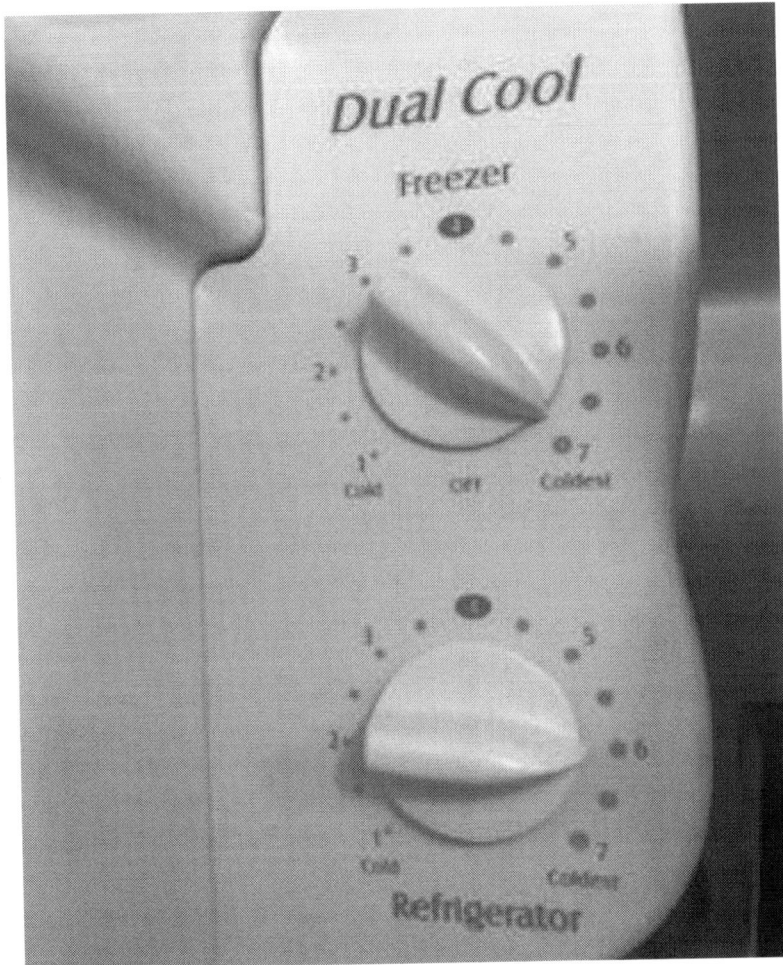

Freezer set on Highest Setting at Home only on Capping

days. Turn back down when you are done cold capping.

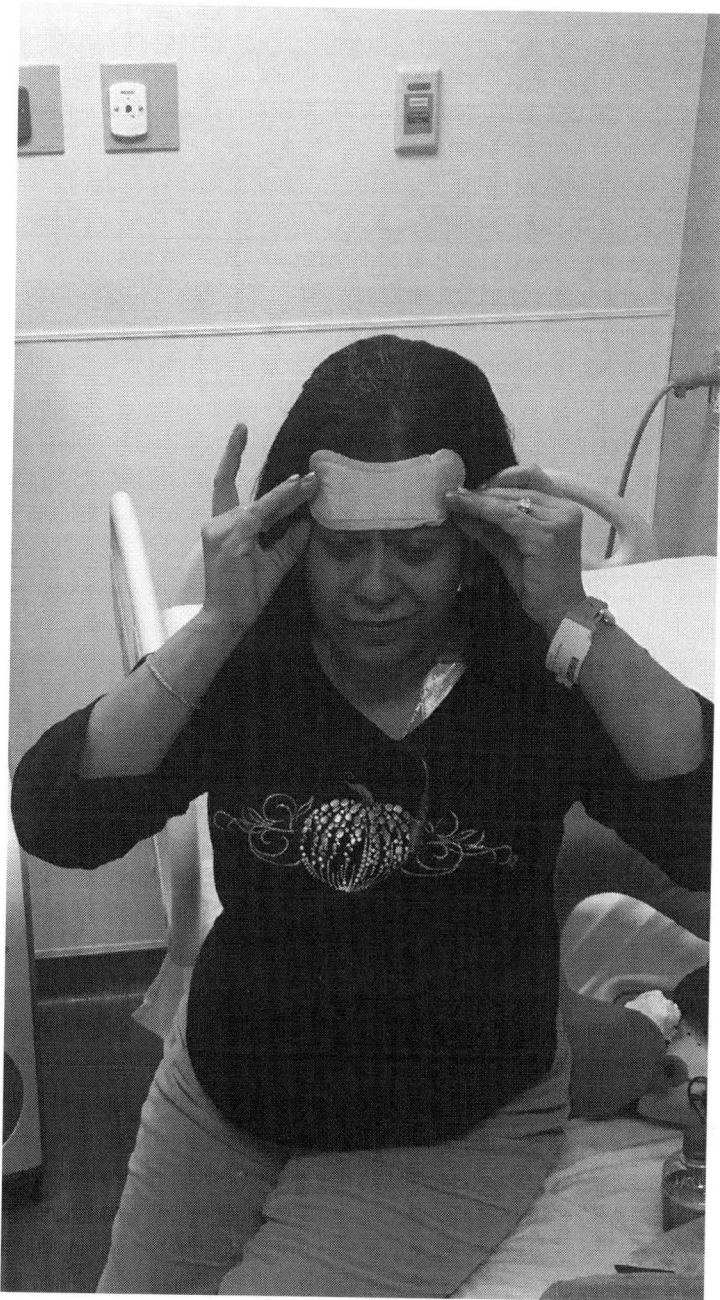

Cover your forehead and ears with a pad to prevent them from getting cold during you cold capping sessions.

CHAPTER 2
PLAN AHEAD

Plan financially, 3 months ahead. Start a Go Fund Me page, to get financial help for your journey. Try to raise at least $1,000 on your campaign. I raised money for myself. I was pleasantly surprised with all of the support that I received. It restored my faith in humanity.

To do List:

Items to buy and things to do.

1. Gel Caps Online- I got the Small/Medium.
2. Temperature Laser online.
3. Eye cooling mask.
4. Find DRY ICE in your area. Call grocery stores, they carry it.
5. Purchase a cooler with wheels on it.
6. Brush with only a Soft toothbrush and baking soda toothpaste. This will prevent sores so that you will be able to eat.

7. Get your teeth Cleaned before you start your very 1st infusion as to cut down on mouth sores.

8. Purchase and research these vitamins on Amazon. They have literally saved my life and eased the symptoms.

9. My 2nd Round of chemo was not as bad as the first

   while taking these supplements (Pure Graviola)

   Please research this also, it's called soursop online and

   the benefits of breast cancer. However, I'm not a

   doctor but this has worked for me and I was asked

   by several ladies to share my experience on how I

   kept my hair during chemotherapy. Also, with minimal side

   affects.

10.   Purchase a water bottle with drink markers. Stay hydrated and pee the chemo OUT!

11.   Gel Caps buy 5 to 6 for continuous capping Day 1 of chemo cap day and night the first day...Also, Pure Graviola, Saved my life!!!!! This is the Secret...Please Research this supplement online.

Products to buy Cont.:

Pure Graviola is saving my life...please read the reviews online...My wonderful new daughter in-law told me about this...In my opinion, I think that Pure Graviola shrunk my tumor and curbed my chemo side effects. In my opinion, that is. I mean my lab work measured my tumor at 2.5 cm and when it was removed it was 2.2 cm. Those are just the facts.

I took 3 of the pure graviola per day and the day before my Chemo, but not the day of Chemo. In my opinion, The supplement Graviola: Curbed my side effects. Shout out to my daughter in law for suggesting this...I Love you Dominique.

For Shiny and Strong and Healthy Hair During Chemo.

Recommendations:

Hair Pills:

Bamboo Root and Horsetail

These are my further recommendations.

Heating Pad for bone Pain and body aches...and pain meds from your doctor. Again, this is what worked for me. So, consult your physician first before taking any kind of pills, vitamins or medications.

CHAPTER 3
Bone Pain and Body Aches

After your first treatment, you will start to experience

bone pain and body aches, due to the On-Body Injector that

will be administered. It is an at home, shot in your arm,

automatically delivered to your arm (duration 1 hour of

delivery of medicine to arm) the day after chemotherapy

treatments. After the medicine has been administered into

your arm. For about an hour. You can remove it from

your arm...gently take the tape off and it will come off. The

doctors will tell you that allergy medicine will help with the

Bone Pain and body aches. If Allergy medication doesn't work,

then I suggest that you advocate for yourself and ask for pain medication like I did. Please advocate for yourself. The doctors want you to.

Make sure that you tell your doctors about all of your symptoms and ask for a different medication if the ones that you are taking do not work for you...DO NOT SUFFER IN PAIN AND TELL NO ONE...

There are support groups to help you emotionally as well. There are ladies on chat sites, blogs and apps that have been on there for years and have seen a lot and can offer you a lot of good advice...Chat lines, blogs or apps are also amazing for emotional support. I really needed it when I signed up. **Only people with Breast Cancer truly know how you feel**. This is what I was told.

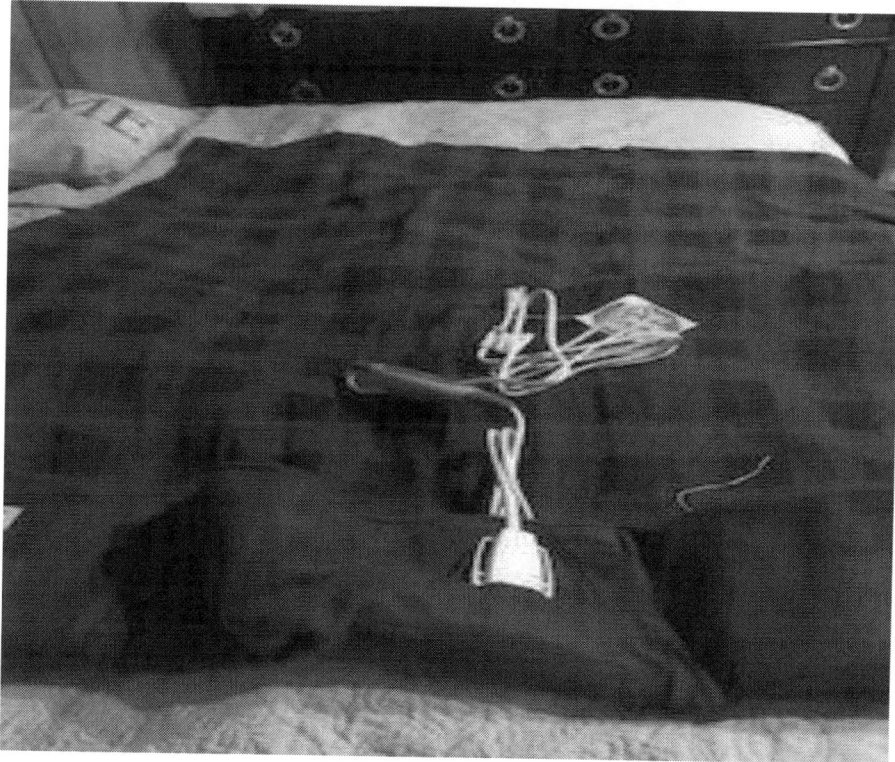

Use a heating throw for bone pain. Wrap yourself up in

It. Bone pain hurts. Ask for pain medication if you cannot take

the bone pain...Most doctors will not refuse at least 5mgs of

some type of pain medication.

CHAPTER 4
WHY DO THEY STARE WHEN I SAY THAT I'M ON CHEMO?

If you are cold capping, then people will assume that you are not that sick. Well this is the only downfall to capping. You are, indeed, still very sick but you will have the Quality of Life that does not broadcast it to the world, that you are sick. You will not look like a woman with breast cancer because you will still have your hair. This is misleading and people will be confused by it...You can just say that I am cold capping to keep my hair. Cold capping was approved in the USA in 2017 and has been used for over 2 Decades in EUROPE. Why are we so afraid to try to figure this out. It's not rocket science. Just use a cold cap before, during, and after treatment for up to 2 days up until your body cools down from the HOT Chemo.

Your body will be hot, and your head will be frying if you don't cool yourself down...hence the hair loss and chemo brain.

My hair stylist says that none of my hair came out. I also, Never EVER Lost the CROWN of my hair during my whole battle with breast cancer like ALL of the others in my caner group. So maybe I have cracked the Science on this cold capping thing, and so I wish to share it with the rest of the world.

Picture Gallery:

Infusion- Round 2 of Treatment AC Still no hair loss.
AC Adriamycin (Red Devil) Chemo
(D- Day) Hair Expected to fall Out.

CHAPTER 5
D-Day

D-Day is: Your 2nd Round of Chemo - Day 2- Hair is

Expected to: Fall Out on this day, all on the Pillow.

With cold capping, one misconception is that you should stop

cold capping once you leave the hospital, but this is not true.

(Secret) You must continue to cold cap ALL Day on Chemo

days up until the wee hours or whenever you HOT

FLASH**...** So, the takeaway here is, COLD CAP for 2

Days after each and every treatment...do not

allow your head to get hot on chemo days 1 and 2...Cap

periodically during this time on eye lashes and eyebrows as

well. This means wearing a Gel Cap or some type of cooling hat for the entire day and the day after.

Trial Study #1

This is what happened to me... Clinical Notes Day 1:

8:40 am...no tingling in my head means no Chemo has reached my Brain...I stayed up and Cold Capped from 5pm, when I got home from treatment, until 4am the next morning. On and off for about 3 hours, or whenever I got HOT, or got a hot flash. I would grab a cap out of the freezer whenever I felt the top of my head getting hot, or HOT flashes.

P.S. Chemo causes hot flashes, but you probably already figured this lol. Check the temperature on the cap first before you use it. The cap is safe between a negative 10 and negative 32

degrees coming out of your freezer or dry ice.

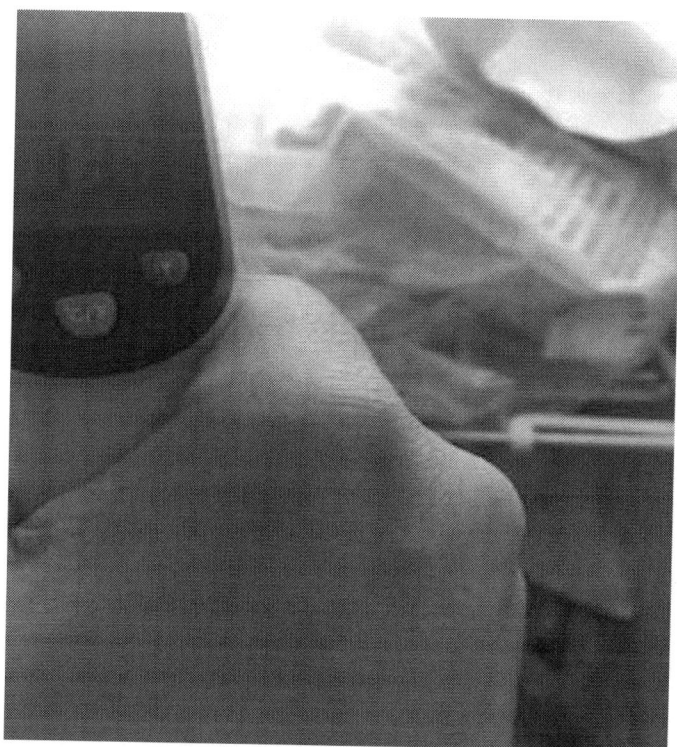

Get those cold cap bags in the Freezer...Put one on your hair

when the temperature reaches -10 degrees to positive

numbers at home just for cooling. Maybe -10 – +20 degrees

when cold capping at home...Cold Capping feels good. You will

get so hot on Chemo days that it will actually, make you feel better because the Chemo is not reaching, touching, or FRYING

YOUR BRAIN!!!!

Hence the word Chemo Brain. I don't want to know what

chemo brain is, but it sounds terrifying, and I wanted no

part of that. I won't even Google that. I just hear the chemo

brain stories from other patients. They say that the chemo has

fried their brain. But doctors say that this is only temporary and

that it will get better.

Research and Data Findings

Trial Study. #1. AC- Adriamycin – Red Devil Chemo

I did the same procedures in the 1stClinical Trial that I did

In the 2nd Clinical Trial and none of my hair came out.

1st Infusion cold capping days not recorded but done.

Although it is not recorded here...I cold capped on my 1st Day of

Infusion Treatment and 2 days after my 1st Infusion treatment...

I Started recording my results after the 2nd Round of Adriamycin

Chemotherapy.

2nd Chemo infusion Day - Capping Schedule at Home.

Remember cap for up to 2 days.

Infusion Day- Day 1 of Post Capping when you get home:

Clinical Notes:

This was my POST at HOME capping Schedule Post/after the

use of the Hospital cold capping machine.

With the use of the Gel Caps purchased online.

4:30 PM - Put on Gel Cap, in the car, 30 min.

5:30 PM - Cold Capped 30 min. on and off, or whenever either

my body, **or the TOP of My Head gets hot. (The Science)**

until the cap gets cold. I capped until Midnight...

2nd Infusion Day- Day 2 - Continue to Cap
CAPPING EVENTS RECORDED

Clinical Notes: AC Adriamycin- Red Devil Chemo

10:00 am 30 min. I capped for 30 min. eyes and brows.

Rub or lightly dab mustard seed oil on brows and lashes.

10:40 am – Capped 30 min. or until the cap gets cold.

5 seconds on eyes and lashes and brows. Put cold packs

on your eyes periodically, for several seconds, for about

1 hour.

11:00 am – 30 min. Cold Capped

12:00 noon Cold Capped

Switching out cap bags in my freezer...

Hot Flash- Cold Capped at 1:36 PM Until the cap gets

warm.

Be Sure to: Cap all Hot Flashes on Days 1 and Days 2 – This is the Science and why it works.

You will **NOT** need to cap on day 3 after your Chemo treatments. But you are still in your hot 7-day cycle. Let me explain. From the day that you start chemo and up to 7 days, you will be on your hot 7-day cycle. And the following week, you will be on your cold 7-day cycle on no chemo.

On day 7 (your cold week, no chemo week) you can style or blow dry your hair. Your scalp will be cold on day 7. Choose either cool or warm settings for seconds at a time...no heat on the scalp. No holding the dryer close to the scalp.

Remember that the best thing that you can do as a cancer patient is cold cap before, during, and after treatments...This means Capping up to 2 days after treatment...Your body will be hot on the day of treatment, and cooling your scalp and body down will just feel so good and relaxing. When your hair follicles are frozen to -32 degrees (which does not hurt at all and actually feels good and cool) the chemo does not get a chance to reach the Brain.

So, in my opinion, capping can also prevent Chemo Brain as well. I'm writing 2 books while on Chemo, so, my brain has not been affected and this procedure worked for me. Chemotherapy fries your brain. So, cool your brain down whenever you feel either your body getting hot, or the top of your head getting hot. This is the science behind cool capping. It must be done continuously for 2 days post every single treatment.

This is the misconception as to why it is not working for so many women. I cannot say it enough, it won't hurt to try it...Cold cap for 2 days ladies...Chemo day, and the day after. After that, your head will be cool to the touch in 7 days. Until then do not touch, comb, or style your hair. Let it lay flat with a small part down the middle of your hair. After day 7 of treatment. I was able to blow dry my ends a little on HOT, just to get the ends straight. But only on non-treatment week (COLD WEEK) ...During Treatment week (HOT WEEK) wait 7 days to touch or style your hair.

Again, no combs, or brushes at all...fingertips only (SECRET)!! Also, do not TOUCH ROOTS AT ALL, WHILE on CHEMO or when styling at all...No ROOT TOUCHING

EVER!!!!! I will be repeating a lot of information in this book that is extremely Important to keeping your hair and if I repeat it, then it is because it has never been said online (in my opinion).

Run water through your hair in the shower to get your hair straight...or get your hairstylist to run the water through your hair. No scrubbing, **just let the force of the water wash and straighten the hair. Get a deep conditioner first but air-dry the deep conditioner**. You may go under the dryer on warm and not hot.

Only go under the dryer for warm hair drying, and only 1 time while at the salon. Only a pea size of product only to lay down your hair and fly always. Pea size hair gel afterwards to lay down fly a way's only. No oil in or on your scalp at all.

Part a small part, down the middle of your hair as to not stress

the hair. Not all the way back, but a 1-inch part in the center.

Put a 100% silk scarf on it, and leave it alone...Fingertips

only...**See watch, like and subscribe to my videos on YouTube.**

My Channel is (sherripade1) for videos on what to do during

your hot week and your cold chemo week.

During your cold week or non-chemo week you can opt

to get your hair gently washed at a salon by a stylist.

The dryer should be set on the cool setting, and your hair

should be put into a loose pony. Again, do not brush comb or

style your hair during your hot week. Only, lightly style or dry

on warm or cool settings on your cold week. Thin hair may not

need to be blow dried. But air dried.

Under the dryer 1 week after 1st infusion...Cold

week...warm setting.

Me, under the dryer scared to death that it might not

work lol....

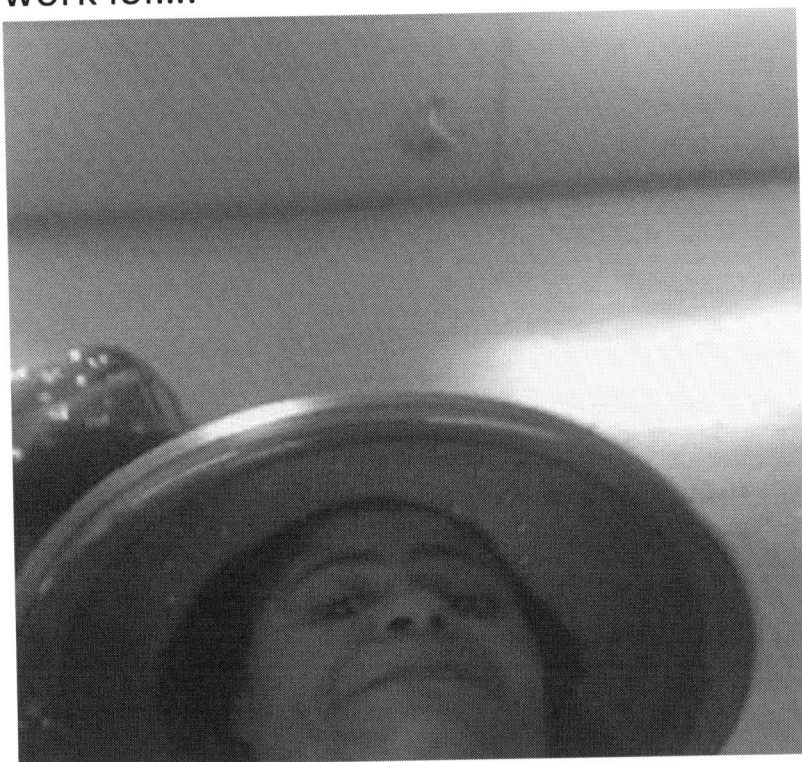

CHAPTER 6
HOW TO STORE AND HANDLE AND DISPOSE OF DRY ICE

You can purchase dry ice from lots of major grocery stores. That's where I purchased mine.

They also sell Dry ice at some hardware stores. Dry Ice will cost around $40.00 and you will need about 30 lbs.

While transporting dry ice in your car. It is important that you leave your back window cracked, or down. Dry Ice is Combustible so DO NOT PUT IT IN THE BACK OF YOUR TRUNK.

You may also dispose of unused dry ice at any Hospital Facility Hazardous materials Receptacle.

CHAPTER 7
HOW TO TREAT YOUR HAIR

How you treat your hair is very important. Do not wash your hair daily as it will truly fall out. Please wait seven days after treatment to gently wash your hair. Use non-paraben and non-sulfite shampoo only. Your hair stylist will have these items. Wear your hair back in a pony tail on Cold Days and wear your hair out and flat with a slight front part in middle on hot Chemo week.

Remember Hot Chemo week is 7 days or your Chemo Treatment Week. Cold Chemo week is the week following Chemo week, when your head is no longer hot and susceptible to root damage. Remember not to run fingers through or touch your roots at all during your hot chemo week. Don't even let your stylist touch the roots. Just say, "let the water straighten. it out in the sink." She must use her hands and fingers only, and NO styling tools, only a small tooth comb to lay it down, a little laying hair down with the small tooth comb may be okay but no COMBING THROUGH THE ROOTS

EVER!!!!!!

Hair Oil – Never grease your scalp. Your scalp is naturally oily so you never need to oil it…. that will clog up your pours…Only oil the ends and hair strands only and not your scalp. Greasing your scalp will only clog your pours and stop hair growth.

Not putting enough oil on your hair is also not good for your hair as well…Dry and brittle hair will break so oil the ends of your hair…I like to say "Feed the Ends of your hair" with oil….

Me Round 2 of AC/Adriamycin (Red Devil) Chemo

...Still no hair loss.

CHAPTER 8
YOUR BREAST CANCER RESOURCES

1. Here is a list of Resources that I have found useful.
2. Triple Negative Foundations.
3. Copay foundations.
4. Meals on Wheels.
5. BC Healthline App for emotional support chat.
6. Student Loan Cancer Debt Postpone
7. DC, Maryland and Virginia, Washington Area Cold Cap Relief Fund – I got approved for $1,000.00 reimbursement of my cold cap out of pocket expense. Must pay up front though...$700.00 deposit.

CHAPTER 9
PARTING AND STYLING YOUR HAIR WHILE ON CHEMO

While on Chemo you should only wear 2 styles. Hair flat on Hot weeks, and hair in loose back pony on cold week. Do not stress your hair with any other style. No ROOT COMBING, OR ROOT BRUSHING for 3 to 6 months while on Chemo.

Hair is pinned up in the back on cold week and laid flat on hot week. No touching on Hot Week and yes, you can go to the solon 7 days after infusion. I go 7 days after my infusion. My infusion is always on a Monday. I get my hair washed and dried on the warm setting at the salon, and then fingered into a loose pony. Or all of my is hair pulled back and off the face. Either style will work. These two styles are great for women who don't have chemo but have stressed hair as well. If your hair is really stressed then these two styles and the styling hair parts are great for you. Just dime size amount of oil rubbed onto hands (3 to 4 drops at a time on the ENDS and strands only...Repeat when hair is still dry) and then rubbed through and on top of hair to lay it down and also reach the ENDS of the hair...no oil on the scalp at all. An oily scalp with clog your pores your pores need to breath. Remember to feed the ends of your hair. Your hair will drink it up. Not your scalp because it is naturally oily and will get oil on its own... Do NOT Grease Your Scalp.... This also works for both men and women who are losing their hair naturally...

1. Silk scarf
2. No greasing the scalp
3. Feed the strands and ends of your hair with oil.

4. Start doing a hot oil treatment after chemo is finally completed.
5. Start doing a protein, biotin and carotin, treatment after chemo is completed.

AC Adriamycin (Red Devil) Chemo

Chemo Hot week wash after 7 days. Lay flat with center front part.

HOT WEEK – Flat

Hair flat and down.

December 2019
Hot week.

Cold Week Pony.

November 25, 2019

Hair back in a loose ponytail. Hair slightly pulled back.

Cold week...hair pulled back in a pony...you can style during

cold week. On hot week do not touch your hair for that week.

Hair pulled back in pony on your cold week.

Using Hospital Cold Capping Machines...Find a Hospital

that has one or uses Gel caps at their Hospital. Both work

the same.

Chapter 10
Benefits of Alkaline Water

Alkaline water is an acid found in the bloodstream.

It is said that alkaline water will starve cancer cells and

balance your PH levels. I only drink Alkaline water

during my Cold week and not during my hot weeks.

Please research this on your own. H20, Drink at least 8

cups of water a day or 32 oz. to stay hydrated.

Reminder: PEE IT OUT!!! PEE IT OUT!!!

Pee out the CHEMO!!!!!!

Purchase a water bottle with Drink Markers to keep you

hydrated.

CHAPTER 11
YES, YOU CAN SEE YOUR HAIRDRESSER WHILE ON CHEMOTHERAPY

POST 2ND INFUSION COLD WEEK HAIRDRESSER WEEK-

Find a good hair stylist 3 months before you start

treatment, to train your hair to be pulled back. As it will

be in this state for about 6 to 9 months. Wash your hair only

weekly and only during your cold week.

Never wash your hair 3 days before or 3 days after

chemo treatment. Remember on Hot Weeks hair is flat

for cold capping. Do not pile hair on top of your head

while capping. Leave hair alone in the scarf for 1 week.

On cold weeks, wear your hair in a loose ponytail in the

back and leave it alone for 1 week. Notes to tell your

hairstylist. Lukewarm or cool water on the scalp. No

direct heat to the scalp ever. May blow-dry ends of hair.

Do not root dry, or root touch, or root pull your hair.

Again, no combing from the roots, for 6 months of

treatment...This is the key to keeping your

roots tight during chemotherapy treatment.

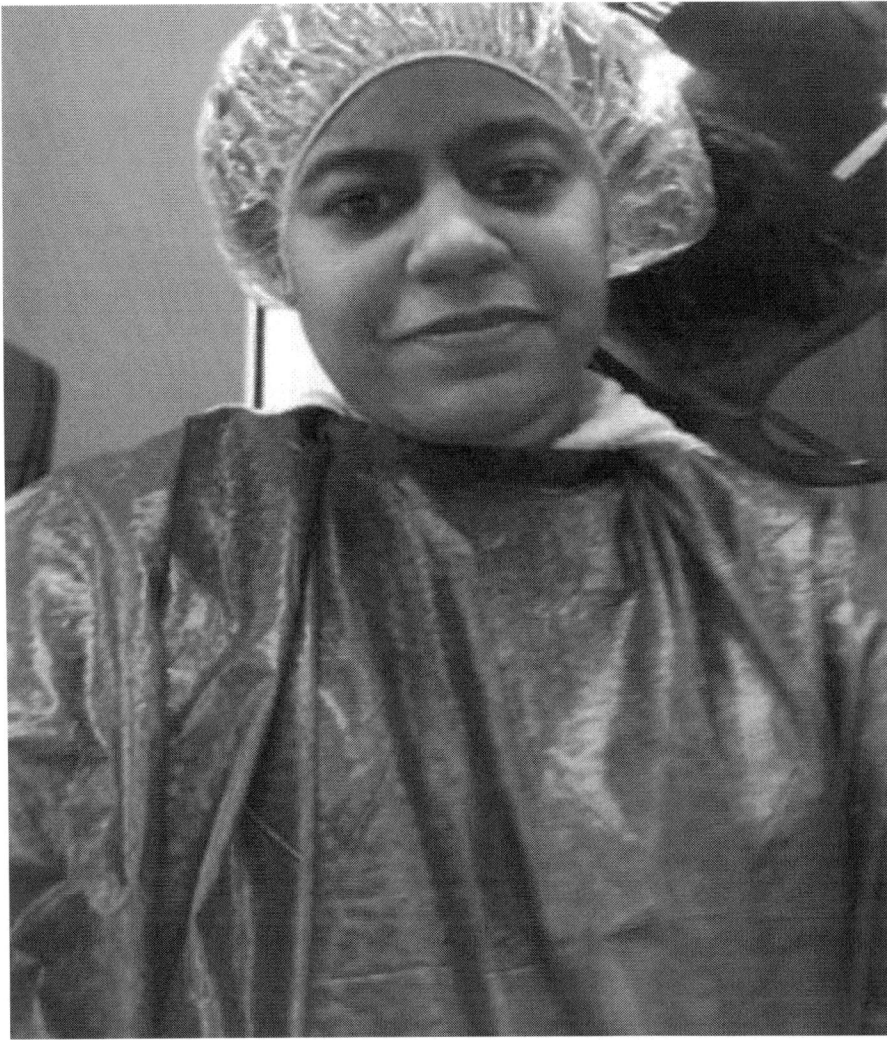

January 2020 still no hair loss.

Let the flow of the water push hair back in the sink.

When drying from the hair dryer, only finger untangle, only...

Use fingers to untangle the hair only when it has dried

Completely.

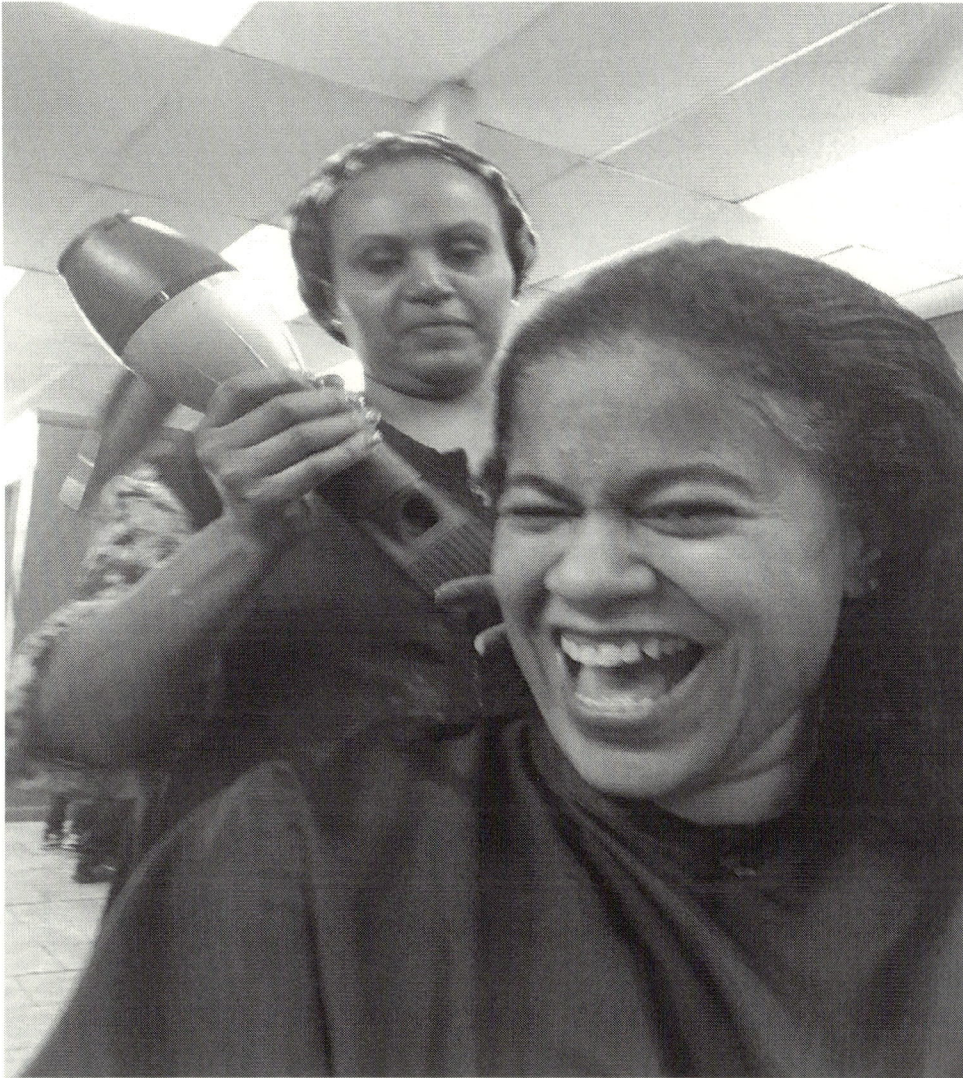

On a warm setting. Blow dry the middle and ends

only...No root touching, or pulling...

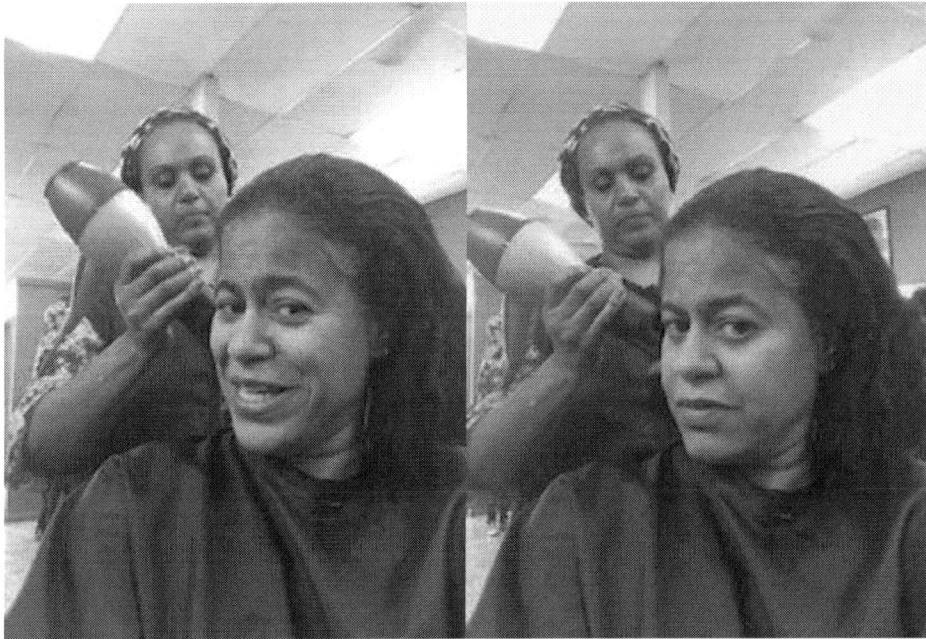

It's working, but I'm still scared to death, lol...Remember, this

is a trial experiment. Cold Week: Scarf under cap. 100%

Silk scarf, no cotton or polyester. The scarf is used to o prevent

constant movement or stress of hair while capping for 2 days.

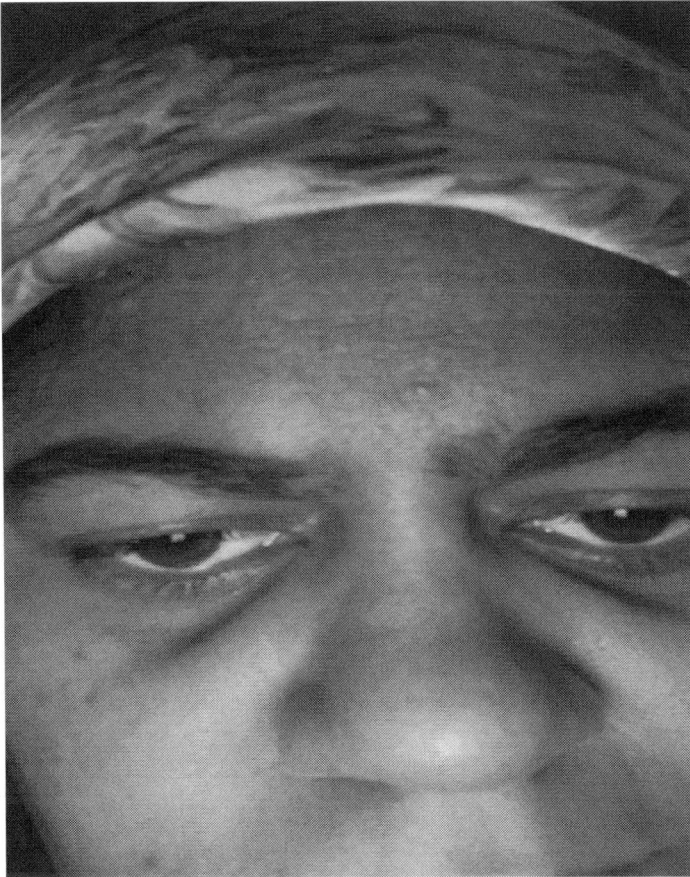

Capping my eyes and face. I still have all of my facial hair.

Brows and eyelashes from capping them with ice on days 1 and

2.

Must Haves! Please research this Vitamin Soursop.

Use daily: Baking Soda toothpaste to prevent sores on tongue or in mouth. Use a soft toothbrush only. Do not use medium bristle toothbrushes or hard bristle toothbrushes. Soft ONLY! I never got mouth soars like some people. Be sure to get your teeth cleaned 3 months before your first infusion.

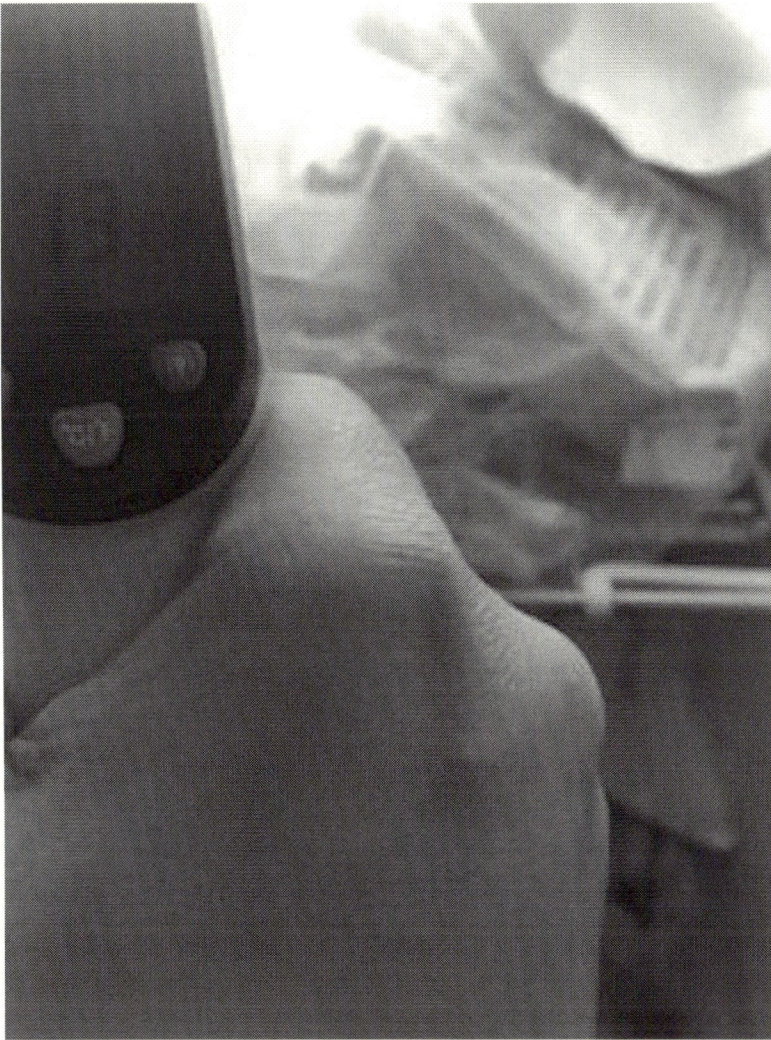

Keep Cold Caps at home in your freezer on the very

highest temperature on Capping day. Turn freezer down

on non-capping days.

Cold Week hair pulled back.

AC Adriamycin (Red Devil) Chemo

Still no hair loss…Hot week…hair is out to breath and be free.

Keep hair in a 100% silk scarf. They only cost $13.00.

Hot Week

NO ROOT TOUCHING, PULLING, OR COMBING!!!!!

Veggie Soup or chicken and rice soup under 800 -850 grams of sodium.

Quick Reminder: While transporting dry ice from the store **DO NOT PUT DRY ICE IN THE TRUNK OF YOUR CAR!!!!! DRY ICE IS COMBUSTIBLE!!!!!**

Keep dry ice in plastic bags. Use gloves. Let bags breathe

a little…DO NOT SEAL ANY DRY ICE BAG they already

come with holes poked into them. Leave the

prepackaged dry ice alone. Let it stay in the prepackaged bags.

Stick a small bag of dry ice into caps. Make sure caps stay inside

of the bags while they are in the freezer or in the cooler. I keep

my cooler outside at all times with the dry ice outside as well.

Feb. Valentine's Day
Still no hair loss...

March

Still no hair loss...

CHAPTER 11 TAXOL

The second round of chemo will be Taxol.

Now this chemo had a slightly different affect on my

hair. The ends of my hair needed to be trimmed at the

very tips. The ends got really dry and brittle so just cut the

ends of your hair and keep it combed out every day...you

must comb the ends of your hair every day...this is very

important while taking Taxol. The ends of my hair

became very brittle so I had to trim the ends of my hair. I still

NEVER LOST THE CROWN OF MY HAIR. Wait till day 10 to wash.

So, while my hair did have no effect with the red devil

Chemo. Taxol was different, but my hair still never fell

out...I never, ever lost the crown of my hair. But because I didn't have my long hair, I continued to wear a scarf and I ordered lots of news boy hats in different colors. I also had very few symptoms while on Taxol chemo. Just changes in my hair texture, which will return to normal 4 weeks after Taxol. You will **not** have to start your hair from scratch because you will not go bald. Your hair will be back to its normal length in 3 to 4 months and not the 1 year that it would take if your hair were to completely fall out. Taxol wash after 10 days and not 7 days...Post 6 week after ALL chemotherapy treatments be sure to use a hot oil treatment, and protein hair treatment every week, to restore your natural hair and get it strong and healthy again. You may now put a perm or color in your hair...I am African American, so I use one for Black People...But keep up a healthy clean hair routine of washing, hot oil and deep condition every week or every Sunday.

CHAPTER 14
RADIATION THERAPY EASY ROAD

Now that you are in radiation therapy, you will finally

see the road at the end of the tunnel. You will have to go

every single day for 29 days in a row...That is, weekdays I mean

to say. But it will go by fast...you will get cream to use from

your doctor. Be sure to apply the protective cream 5 hours

before your treatment and 1 hour after your treatment...that

will be 2 times a day. This will prevent burns and protect the

area from getting burned during radiation therapy.

Week 4 your breast will be sensitive...do not wear a bra

at home and only were a sports bra on your way to

Radiation. No wire bras and no deodorant under the arm

of radiation. As much as possible just let your breast

breathe and hang. Use the creams that they give you at the hospital for minor radiation burns or itching.

You are now, almost at the end of your journey...

Remember to Stay strong and keep your appointments and always follow your doctor's orders.

CHAPTER 15
ONE YEAR OF YOUR LIFE COMPLETELY GONE
AND THIS TOO SHALL PASS

Well you have spent at least 9 months to one year in

and out of the hospital, going back and forth to doctors'

appointments, and it is almost over. Stay positive, and

always have a bright, uplifting, and positive attitude, and

you will get through this in a breeze. Reach out for help

when you need to, and don't be afraid to ask for help. It is

the key to helping some people get over a lot of

depression...Ask for help, if you need it...You don't HAVE TO

SUFFER ALONE...GOD DID NOT PUT US ON THIS EARTH TO

SUFFER ALONE...PLEASE JUST ASK....

So...

To Re-Cap...REMEMBER TO...

POST CAP, at Home, the day of Treatment and the day after.

Capping for 2 days is the science ladies...That is the Key

and the Secret that they don't want you to know.

This book is dedicated to Rick...the love of my life...we

have been through so much together. You have seen

me at my best, and you have seen me at my worst...you

have always been a shoulder to lean on, my rock to

hold on to and to keep me steady. I adore, and admire you,

forever and always...

You are the Love of my Live,

Sherri...

THANK YOU TO MY WONDERFUL FRIENDS AND FAMILY WHO
HELPED ME THOUGH THIS TOUGH TIME IN MY LIFE...HOW DO I
JUST LOVE YOU SO MUCH FOR ALL OF YOU HELP AND
SUPPORT...

Picture Gallery 2019-2020:

**Through My 1 Year with Breast Cancer. Thank you, to my
Family, Coworkers and Friends**...

My Wonderful Son and I....

My Amazing Son, Victor. Love you so much...

My Handsome son Victor.
2019

My beautiful daughter in-law Dominique...Kisses....Love you to pieces....

My dad and I. Me cold capping Lol...I Love you dad...

Smooches...

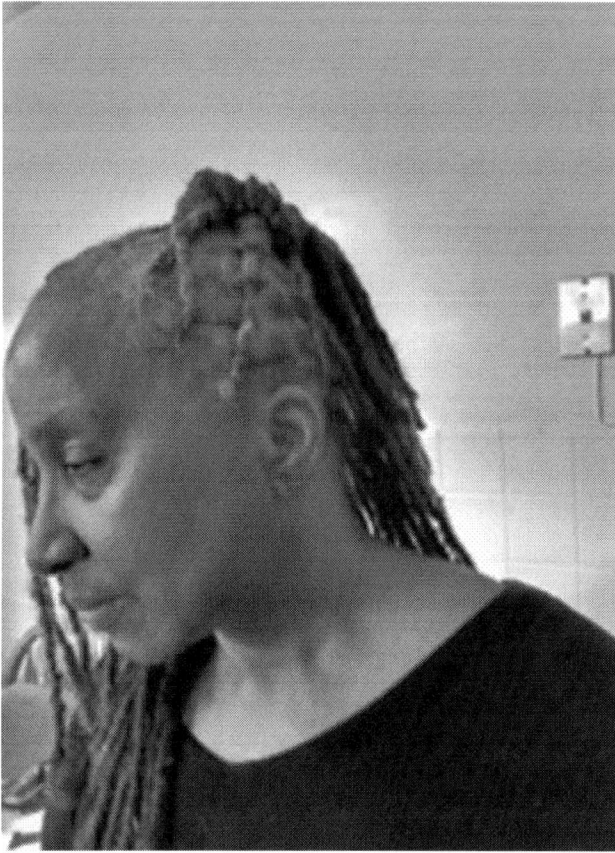

My beautiful Stepmom Francis

My brother Nick

Grandma and Grandpa...

My brother and best friend Terron .

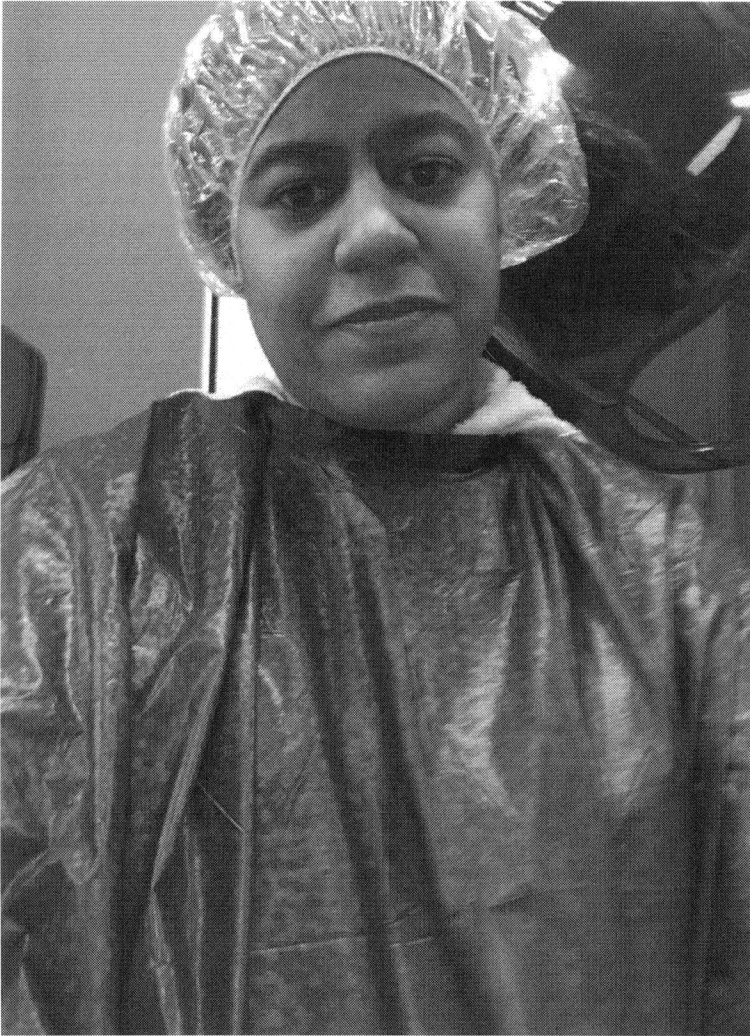

At the hair salon...during chemo treatments....

At home...my skin is so pale...Look brows are fading away but still there almost...Still have all of my root hair and hair length...

My sister...Leigh Leigh...I Love you to pieces...

My Bestie Danette. Love you sis...

My Mom...Denise Paden, I Love to so much....

Covid-19... Still went to Chemo treatments...

Getting my hair done while on chemo. Thanks Ozzie, my hair

Stylist.

Thanks to Ozzie, my beautiful hair stylist...

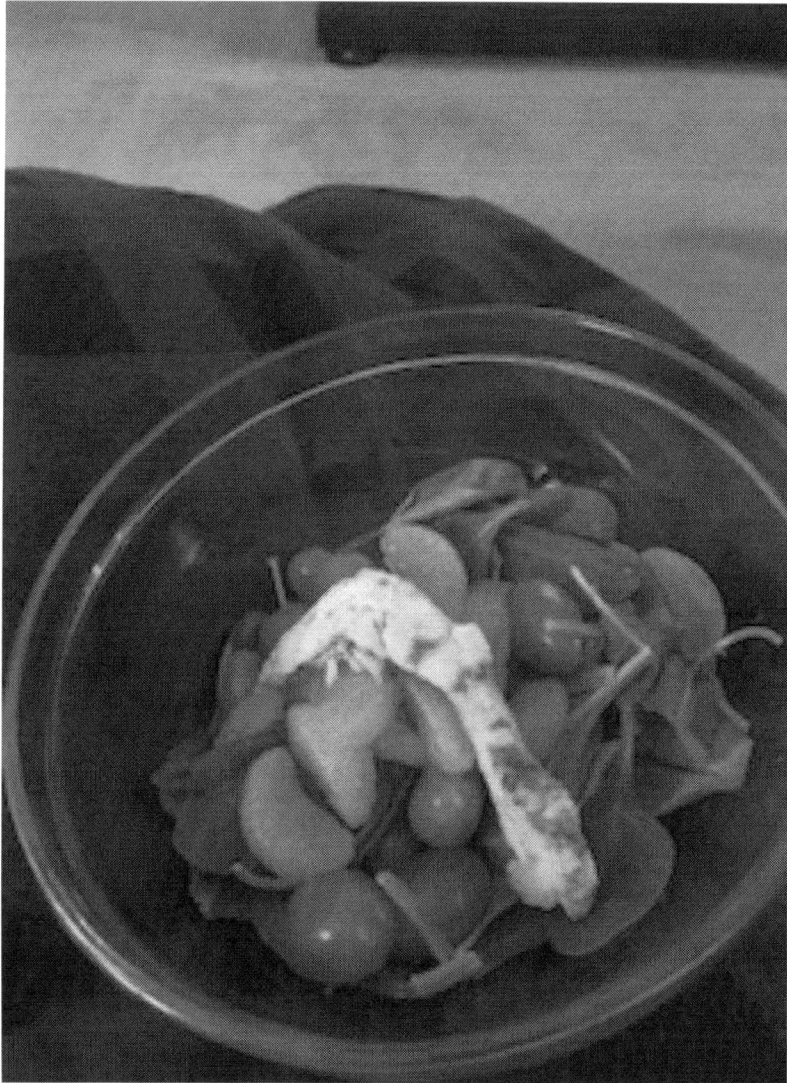

Eat only bland food that you can stomach and take anti-nausea medication. Take 2 the night before chemo treatment and 1 the morning of chemo treatment.

In ending, I hope that writing this book has inspired you to keep your hair and also, to Keep Your Quality of Life!!!

We don't have to lose our hair ladies. Stay Positive and Stay Blessed and Let's all just keep up the fight in Our Breast Cancer Journey...

Until next time...Stay Truly Blessed!!

References: Click on Links to Guide You
http://www.rapunzelproject.org/coldcaps.aspx

 Amazon.com
https://www.amazon.com/gp/product/B07CZDCKN3/ref=ppx_y
o_dt_b_asin_title_o00_s00?ie=UTF8&psc=1

YouTube Channel sherripade1
https://www.youtube.com/watch?v=7ZGTVo7ld0g&t=11s

ELASTO GEL CAP

Southwest Technologies CAP602 Elasto-Gel Cranial Cap
Large/XL

Swanson

Swanson Horsetail Hair Skin Nails Beauty Urinary Tract
Support Supplement 500 mg 90 Capsules

Swanson Bamboo Extract for Hair and Nails Silica
Supplement Supports Collagen 300 mg 60 Veggie
Capsules

PAXMAN CORP.- https://www.paxmanusa.com/

http://www.rapunzelproject.org/

https://penguindryice.com/

https://ww5.komen.org/

**Cancer: Is Alkaline Water a Treatment Option? -
Healthline**

Eye mask cooling:
https://www.amazon.com/gp/product/B07QG9Y5B3/ref=ppx_y
o_dt_b_asin_title_o04_s00?ie=UTF8&psc=1
Neck pillow:

https://www.amazon.com/gp/product/B00IPPA73C/ref=ppx_yo
_dt_b_asin_title_o05_s00?ie=UTF8&psc=1

Disclosure: The opinions of this author are from my own
experience…Please consult your doctors beforehand.

The END

Sherri M. Paden

2/2020

60195042R00069